Miss Manhattan

Miss Manhattan

BIMAN ROY

ARPress
ILLUMINATING IDEAS
EMPOWERING VOICES

ARPress
45 Dan Road Suite 5
Canton, MA 02021

Hotline: 1(888) 821-0229
Fax: 1(508) 545-7580

Ordering Information:
Quantity sales. Special discounts are available on quantity purchases by corporations, associations, and others. For details, contact the publisher at the address above.

Printed in the United States of America.

ISBN-13:   Softcover   979-8-89389-225-3
                eBook   979-8-89389-226-0
                Hardback   979-8-89389-227-7

Library of Congress Control Number: 2024906328

TABLE OF CONTENTS

''The glories strung like beads on my smallest sights and hearings, on the walk in the street and the passage over the river,''

from Crossing Brooklyn Ferry

Walt Whitman

"Dedicated to all New Yorkers"

Geography of Bliss

An old Indian trail becomes *Heere Straat,* then
Breede Wegh on the face of a peevish map
poorly imitating Lisbon, now runs across your body
like an artery carrying a myriad of memory molecules
right into your sleep, and you wake up sometimes
dry-throated, asking for relief or something
similar, then flee to the nearest bar, airport,
hotel lobbies on the farthest to look
for a geography of bliss, or hope to meet a trickster,
a chorus girl, or even a retired gangster,
if there is anything like that, who might offer
you a sip of bootlegged booze to levitate.
Then you give up and try to hide in a narrow crater.

Only Here

Superheroes are born in New York

because of skyscrapers and elevated rails,

as their imagination soars high up

or so I have been told by some introvert scholars,

most of them having immigrant parents

look for a phosphorescent

aspiration of exciting height.

When I walk in the shade of a side street,

a pizza deliveryman bicycles past my dreaming self

with a red and blue cape, and a young woman

wearing a blooming magnolia blouse bends over

through her second-floor window and reads

from *War and Peace* loudly to the crowd below,

to bring back mystery and magic

to her stuffy apartment of fear.

A man walking in front of me calls his dog Robin

and waits until he is done and wraps it in polythene

like precious Kryptonite, and at Union Square

the new mayor promises the world to his citizens

despite war and Washington.

Here an Albanian boy and a Creole speaking girl

meet for the first time in the E train from Queens

and on a day when trees on the sidewalk turn color,

he holds her close, looks up at the sky, and says,

Help us, Superman.

And the girl's singing breasts—

far more sweet-sounding than a lyre,

golder than gold.

A Reason for Language

Contrived or not, the East Side truly believed that the West

Side robbed their muslin and ardor

imported from the Far East

and tricked the town with the theatrics of Broadway politics.

As the Parisians poo-pooed the upstart, artistic drive

of New Yorkers when *Guernica* adorned MoMA's wall,

an American battleship torpedoed the singing fish

on the Ninety-sixth Street

dock to silence *Die Wacht* Am Rhein for treason.

And going by

the toothless fishmonger of Fulton Street and the bootless mayor

of the East Village who owned a bookstore meant for dummies

next to a place for fancy rubber. Words are meant to be shaped,

sucked, and tongued over again and again, then blown into bubbles

of vibrant Corning glass and placed with utmost care between

tear and a tear, but some might float up and come down

to settle on grass, grit, or clergymen's hurrying robes

to become New Yorkese that you carry lovingly to your lover.

Some might walk silent to an uptown mall or to a ball in Queens

or chase a firecracker all the way to Camden to wander and ponder

in the contemplation area named after Walt Whitman.

Tribeca

White of lilies hanging low from shy clouds,

make nights look more mysterious—

like Cavafy and his sublime, young songs.

Being chosen means nothing except a glint of determination—

here I am standing in line for an Italian entry

into Tribeca with two young ladies who are

as mysterious as apple blossoms in a faraway farm

under a nameless tree's abundance of verdant leaves.

The festival tends to bring back the economy

of downtown, a De Niro dream, and it did

in slow sale of fads, fabric, and food—

a feather in Cinema's cap.

I find myself in the mind of the film,

the city hovers in the background

like a girl pirouetting in a short, pink skirt,

tender and unabashed, pleat by pleat.

Frida's Garden

In Frida's garden,

everything is possible:

the blue moon, the blue house with blue doors.

Inside,

stranded birds of desire,

pigments of prickly pears,

and an intense indigo
around the thorn necklace.
At nightfall,
strands of loose light
settle upon branches of jacaranda
laced with sweet lavender.

Not too far under the low, stone bridge,
the Bronx River (or a thin shadow of it)
and an infantry of oaks leaning toward
night over azalea bushes.

A shadowy presence crowds at times

with winged insects and dead humming birds;

an Aztec blessing,

lady's eardrops hang

between light and light.

As I drive out through pink

flesh of cut-open fruits

and womb-like flowers ripe with life,

a man in tatters who claims to be

the Storefront Mayor of Fordham Avenue

waves at me.

Picasso at the Park

Always wildness creeps into the shrubs.

Those delineated, cryptic apartments

overlook the streets;

wind over the Hudson instills hope of an afterlife

as night moves closer in ponderous steps.

There is an abundance of women—

seated woman, kneeling woman, standing woman,

woman with a vase, woman with a leaf,

bust of a woman, head of a woman—

scattered in between a few wandering animals—

a cat, a cock, a goat, an owl—and glasses of absinthe,

a violin and a guitar, signs of life on earth

stopped short of *Amen.*

They share secrets with nods and whispers.

Once the light dims and footsteps of curators

fade like the distant drone of a plane out of Kennedy,

they take the stairs; no one speaks

while the tense argument of air reigns

three floors below and out onto Fifty-third Street

as night answers, *I am in.*

They hop between parked cars, past flashing lights,

dodging curious cops and stray New Yorkers

with their heads in their briefcases,

in groups and alone until they feel the soft, moist

grass of Central Park,

beyond the suffocating walls, out under the sky.

When light crosses the East River

and amble onto sleepy streets,

they will all be scattered among majestic elms

choosing their brief corner of grief and delight.

Sketches on Subway Steps

i

Pigeons poke around

the cement feet of statues

of bearded men

who fill the history books

to add weightage here,

and there, a dog pissing

on a dogwood tree,

in full bloom.

ii

Between all these trains,

beneath the cavernous avenues,

carrying this burdened mass

from borough to borough—

so much emptiness

11

and so much plenty

side by side!

Lorca must have had a great time here!

III

Sweet cannabis,

man on the park bench

drugged by sunset.

Sweet cannabis,

man on the park bench,

the sunset doped by the man.

Trains hustle, and

blown newspapers

stick to a wall

of tense air.

IV

This bounty of restless drive

from dawn to dusk

weekdays and weekends

No mercy in the red traffic eye.

No air navigates the trees

And a sense of breathlessness

Spreading wings toward Hudson,

New York, come to my lap;

I will soothe you.

Big Town Boys

Budding imageries of overhauled streets

minus the half-baked Mayoral thoughts of the day,

lost in the hinges of a Manhattan summer

but sustained our spirits between noon and moon.

Despite budget crunch and partisan politics,

we, the dreamers and screamers run life like a marathon

under the El over TV anchors and microbreweries

as the city sank a few inches into the Hudson.

Glenn waited in The Grassroots at St. Mark's Place

to show the pictures of Sadhus from Kumbh Mela

and crippled boys begging on the streets of Bombay.

Beyond the buzz of bazaars, the world remains

a sad place, he said between beers.

We are the Big town boys, our certitude

never wavers, our spirits obdurate, our beds,

unmade as night, deepened, and flesh mellowed.

We pluck the stars, swallow one after another,

until we banish the last Socrates from this world.

The Cage

What works for me

is not just the spring sun

on roadside narcissus

nor a few desperate men trying hard to

break open the boxed music

on the opposite side of the

West Fourth Street Courts,

but the rage inside the cage

built with wrought iron

of indomitable spirits

that burns your finger

on the smooth skin

of the basketball

if you are careless.

Sleek, sweaty, neighborhood muscles

causing turbulence in the air

as they swing past from a dribble to dunk;

the crowd clenching the hot, wire fence

roars as they did in Arcadia.

When bodies collided on the concrete

with a bleeding nose,

they rise renewed right after and fly

like arrows from the bow upward

to become success stories.

This is essentially the New York stuff,

a Queens College professor tells me

looking out of a brandy and cigar bar,

with eyes dabbed in dream.

As the day darkens, the stuff lifts

itself up, wafts like barbeque smoke,

and lands on the movie set

of a New York filmmaker—

prosperous to listen,

like an old man.

Reminder

Walking north of Hudson Street,

a brownstone in the sun,

vine-adorned.

I like to imagine a woman

living in it alone by herself

or with a three-year-old

and a snow-white Shiatsu.

And I say,

Open out the grace of your eyes.

So much to see,

can be pleasant and burdensome

at the same time

and becomes a reminder

of a life lived

in absences

without a promise.

and no pretense as well,

until one night the brownstone walks

into your dream

and decides to stay put,

reminding you of your promise and pretense

What would you do then?

Differing Accents

Music floats out through the window—
The Chickering on its mahogany legs
dances to Chopin in consonance.
How invisibly silence surrounds her.
The luscious pink of rose bush, a femme fatale;
foreplay of wind on the Hudson's breast
as the sun sinks behind Jersey City.
Her parents fled Russia to take refuge here,
just as her doorman's parents
fled the South from lynching
to sleep under a trusted blanket,
as long as it would last,
Fireworks set light and heat to the East River
even as a wicked breeze cools the Halloween night
beyond slanders and slights.
Her numbed hands among the hedges

try to feel past injustices her people suffered

and those of others with

differing accents;

She sits up erect, facing night—

having encountered

wants,

accomplish the plan.

How Language Comes into Being

I have yet to find the cruelest morning that refuses

to crack its thickest door of non-assurance to live,

just as the blackest and stupidest rock

in front blocking the narrow outlet to light has

Andy Loves Lisa tattooed

on its face, like *Hope.*

Stuck in time, I travel at the ponded edge of traffic

with two states of mind almost parallel as Kenneth

Koch who liked to be influenced and influence,

yearning for Mozart and Monet, and Shakespeare,

thought of New York, a simple stroke of genious.

It was still the mid-eighties with funky

music and fatal stabbings and a deep desire to be

delivered out of misery by the federal government,

still building a hanging bridge of language

on which people pass signing laughter to each other.

Alone and lonely, in the same breath,

while enjoying the secret knishes on Delancey Street,

I walk up northwest,

strands of music skitter

like resonant pebbles

against water's refusal to surrender,

faced the tyranny of silence.

And in a lower East Side bar, Isaac Bashevis Singer

went looking for a lone trombone to make language happen.

Zen in Manhattan

Coming toward it is like taking

a few steps back from the mirror

and watching how the hands of light

cup your sunken cheek.

Going away means not coming back

to its banks of rotted flesh

but holding its secret in insomniac twilights,

in play or pretense.

A shifting shadow of a swing

in Central Park,

an utter loneliness of early adolescence,

so Manhattan-like.

Hotel Chelsea

I have always lived close to a river,

a different river each time.

Now it's the Hudson.

Sun slants from the east,

air pierced by arrows of buntings

and crests of lapis lazuli

drift slowly shoreward.

Not too far from here—

secret corridors and shadowy foyers

Wolfe-like

foreboding dread,

tales of murder/suicides

splattered on weepy walls.

A Hotel Chelsea of the heart—

where we come to fend

the salt of our meat.

It makes me feel safe and useful

as each night I gather my supple

limbs close to my ribs

at each bend of river and say,

Into desire

I shall come.

Black Out

All evening, the heat

kept both alive and separate,

even the rumble underneath

had quieted.

Earlier, a stream of hats and skirts

rainbowed over the Brooklyn Bridge.

Not even a slice of steamer's beam

had shined in the path of homing pigeons,

and the giantess kept dozing off,

having been sucked out of its blood-light.

At midnight, I opened

the dead refrigerator,

pulled out of its silence

a hunk of watermelon,

and we both ate its cold in candlelight,

and laughing our heads off for fun or nothing.

Walking with Sappho in New York

How easily pigeons get used to Times Square,
like a dog to an abusive master or a child to a cranky sibling.
Habits mean more than bending to the sways
of the wind or accepting steel fixtures in bones.

I walk toward the museum where Pollock drowns
thumbtacks, cigarette butts with thick-thinking paints.

You amble on the asphalt of a strange city like yours,
where a lover's quarrel in a foreign language
makes you feel at home, and a man's torso glistens
from digging ancient treasures or putting a body in
that would leave a hole in his life or make him wiser,
like dark rain crossing a bridge to green mountains.

Life in the city can be hard,

unlike the soggy sawdust of small towns

or muddy snow of upstate,

but you have a way about it, like pirouetting

as a danseuse on the ice wrapping light around,

swimming through night over the Hudson.

As you walk homeless into the cold of Hell's Kitchen,

you hear inside of you—

I used to weave crowns.

Diagonal Descent

He was on our minds like a patch

of stalking cloud atop the bridge

as we sloped down to Flatbush

and Fulton against the artillery of light.

We walked across the wind,

cold as the accusing glance

of a loved one, until the falafel stand

and a quick meal on the go.

Evening seemed slanted,

but the flow was right

near the trash can row at the curb,

clematis hugging the pole.

It was all about Rimbaud in New York,

Bob Dylan, Patti Smith, and us;

even David's mask

pictured all over the city,

nineteen seventy-eight—

then women danced naked to the bone,

and men played music deep into night.

Aurora borealis descending in the sky,

a grand cosmos was taking a turn.

By the time we came to the landing,

Eros shook my mind

like a mountain wind

falling on oak trees.

A Sky NYPD Blue

Today is Gay Parade Day,

stacked on 364 other important days.

Fifth Avenue looks cute as a cross-dresser.

Glenn is out with his digital—

faces painted green, bodies hugging tight

as in high-school bonding.

My mind is a silver cradle

tipped toward the West Side.

The marchers walk through a field of petunias.

I follow them on the back of a donkey

through apricot clouds

right to the edge of Stonewall.

Today I paint my face suicidal blue.

So, I keep the festoon and drumbeats

close to my skin as an alarm clock

as we are not there yet

to celebrate.

Side Street

All the way from Bleecker

eastward, no sign of live traffic

except a crow holding

onto a dead kitten as ransom,

maybe for the mayor.

Trees heavy with silver studs

languish in the slow shuttle

of a snowy Sunday.

As I shortcut to a narrow street,

the poster of a candidate

for the mayoral race glares at me,

a slut for justice and more penitentiaries

and above it, behind the glass

like a ventriloquist's voice,

Stieglitz's portrait of Georgia O'Keeffe—

fingers gathered around collar

in alluvial tenderness, and

layers of chrome, purple, and magenta

have started a fire on the side street.

In a Gangster's Den

Wind shifting between branches—

still a hot, muggy day in downtown.

Choppers crisscross the blue corridor of sky.

In the basement tunnels

leading to the East River,

I find myself in a gangster's den

with Comrade Trotsky

and rumrunners ready to float

to the Cuban shore.

The speakeasy downstairs

and gallons of bootlegged liquors,

where men simply recorded as missing,

remain well hidden.

Despite shooting on the run,

silent killings on the streets,

gangsters claim to have

their code of ethics:

where speech ends, silence begins;

that is when the plot thickens.

Rumor.

Hair.

At the same time,

man.

Late Spring

Today it's all broken—

the tune that halts at the lip,

the bell that fails to ring at seven,

and your missed phone call,

like an avenue that lost its neon,

Elsewhere, the dusty rafts of tenements

with rotted bones and rags

hung over men with swollen feet

and women with sagging breasts,

children starved of food and love.

The way the other half lives

in the oppressive shadow of concrete confine.

A fetid scent of a singed dream

wafts in the air—

not one of your ordinary mornings

of roasted coffee and bagel.

By afternoon the breaking mellows.

Lining up in cold air at 86 E

for Expressionist paintings,

then sushi and warm sake

in the Village just as life moves on.

Evening comes with Ozu

and his "Late Spring"

bringing back another layer of loss,

like yearning for New York

while living in New York.

In honey voice,

piercing breezes

wet with dew.

One Tattoo at a Time

Painted on the red back of the tourist bus,

onlookers gaze curious, playful,

like a question begging to be asked.

At the corner of Sixth Avenue and Thirteenth Street,

a patch of sunlight on a pigeon's back.

A poodle sits waiting with his master

for the light to change.

Then with two dark spots on its rear

trot away as life moves on

empty-handed.

Almost noon, lunch hour comes as a postman on time.

The town goes to the tattoo parlor,

pigments infuse through rounds and flats,

and the shader bar

moves like a cloud from darkest to lightest.

Then a break, sudden and silent,

like the yard instantly sparrowless,

a suspicion of rain and

imprints of the past inked on the skin

one tattoo at a time.

Do I need that?

nor these,

more around

desire.

That September

At ferry's landing—

cranks of machines cracking marrows

of American lindens fill the air

and at Ground Zero, the eternal digging.

No one knows who tends

the cattle in Ithaca

or who serves coffee in the downtown Starbucks

at these hours

when wind is still as a stroke victim.

The soggy September trench coat

folded in memory of troubadours

is left closed to the street sign bent backwards

and a stench pools around the hydrant.

Walking into the troubled night

of that September

under a traffic-less sky,

I notice on dank pavement a half-rotted root

sinking its teeth into the marrow of Manhattan.

Death, in Any Case

Guess what options one has: either to be shot

right between the eyes or a slow strangle until sunset.

Still, people might choose one over the other depending

what's cooking on the flat-iron skillet of their mind

right then, though someone might say it ain't no choice.

When Stan White was shot

on that champagne-soaked evening on the top tower

of old Madison Square Garden

by a millionaire, (who also stole his red-velvet mermaid

and rode the train gleefully to an insane asylum

in Matawan)

What choices they were handed then,

except settling the score on this side of life?

Often it's a better idea, one might argue, to relocate

one's mind to a private yet public space, as in a Vaudeville, letting the eyes to feast and flesh to simmer

than to prowl the narrow streets of Tenderloin.

Or was it because the girl wanted to flee the boredom

of sameness, or wished to move out of the shadow

of a tree too familiar, or just got swept by the lush lust

of the other man, or was in a bewildered state of mind,

sandwiched between Yes and yes.

Of course, the raucous evenings in downtown lofts can outwait

an armistice, or a slow slithering of a specter of life,

or keeping busy in mindless minutiae, or picking a hobby—

all the usual tricks in the bag to instill stillness

in a windswept, barren land.

But someone might refuse

to choose any, letting the light delicately die inside their eyes.

Keep the Lights On

After all lofts on the Lower East Side were spray painted green,

and the sky ambered under the red balloon floating away,

Bye, she said to her lover, curving slightly at her waist,

Garboesque, and he, with his Stalin moustache, tipped

his pointed hat adieu, in their often-repeated faux parting.

Why not we take a taxi uptown or maybe to Apollo where

De Niro showcasing Taxi Driver? she asked. *I am not sure of that,*

he said while thirsting for McSorley's or any Irish bar in town and

starving for a steak resembling the map of New Jersey.

He wasn't happy, and she was feeling an empty womb

like standing in front of a sexless Warhol splattered across

the silk screen, a siege of the night. But they settled on a

watering hole in the gourmet district before trampling

ahead to Times Square over Reunion's ashes.

Much later, back in the hotel room, in the folds of her lover's arms,

she mumbles, *you know I am afraid of the unknown*

as O. Henry,

Before he died, he wanted the lights to be on to go home.

Unreal City

Sulfur City, its incandescence—

I fell in love with its glint of surreal

when my eyes settled upon from the sky.

I left my husband and my kids

far away in a desolate ranch

with hot days and cool nights—

as in John Wayne movies.

I met the city in the subways, museums,

and bars, trying to map out its contours

and cadence, pushing aside the hopes and fears,

listening to the flourish and flow like two women,

treading their secrets, centuries apart.

While far away, my husband was getting out

of a real car and greeting a real dog

or dropping kids at a real school, I stood with a tree

on a lonely curb drowned in leaves of gold, unreal.

We should have figured each other out by now,

I thought, or maybe not.

And while my husband

was looking at a real watch, I looked over

the bridge, past time and Central Park

to O'Hara leaning breathless on the john door

at the Five Spot, listening to "Strange Fruit" in his head.

Tunnel under the River

Not all lights are turned off yet,
but the dance floor is almost empty.
At the center—a man, a large man
with the face of an army general,
benign and cruel, slowly turning and turning
in a compulsive ritual, and clung to his huge torso,
an immaculate blonde in flowing white
with a crown of live parakeets.

Outside, a chorus girl
walking through artilleries of desire
hurled at her armor of caution
to her man waiting in a taxicab
like the poet from Rutherford
watching from inside for sketching a beauty.
Will he pick her up tonight or any other night

and take her far away,

to Babylon or Alexandria,

through the tunnel under the river?

The Way Things Are

The lady in black stepped out

straight from a Hopper, left

foot first, silk-sheathed and cautious,

onto the rain-washed side street draining into Fifth Avenue.

The man in a green jacket, bald as a cantaloupe,

ran behind and almost tipped over,

balanced himself with a faint smile, and held

the umbrella out, half-opened.

The lady, irate

at the incompetence of night to protect its stars

and vexed at the losing game of Broadway,

asked for a taxi to go far from the piano bar.

The man, sleek as a salesman, craned his neck out

into the pitch-black night

stretched between East River and the Hudson,

and managed to bundle her out to nowhere.

Once she was gone, the man took out a cigar

and smoked as if nothing had really happened—

not even in Hopper's cityscape,

past magic, comedy clubs, heart breaks and filth.

Violet Banks

You stood unpretentious,

between Mott and Baxter on Mulberry Street,

like a tree undressed in fall.

Slant of your face,

warming to the heft

of the morning, reminded me

of rows of green groceries

and funeral parlors.

Beyond the empty park bench,

on the corner stoop, a man or nothing,

like Kafka's desperate letters about letters

to Milena, and I stood struck.

"You fool," I said to myself,

"Why can't you open

like a trumpet or an umbrella?"

Right then, you walked toward me

and leaned in like a ladder,

nimbly whispered,

"Take e to the violet banks."

Sunday, Fall, 7 a. m.

Slow light on low-profiled lily stalks,

an uninterrupted tiger yellow,

a window half closed to a burgeoning day,

like buds of music half opened under a worn

cashmere throw on the antique piano

as side streets slowly court the traffic.

Sunday September blowing past Central Park,

a news train whistles through the Grand Central

like motes of light from another galaxy,

and the heavy musk of sex

permeates the stairwell leading to daylight

and its unfurled, reeling possibilities,

like rows of apartments in Trump's Place

warming up to the Hudson's dawn

as visions of impenetrable blue

at the edge of determined white

makes me feel complete,

even if I die today.

Sunset at the Seaport Inn

At the Fulton Fish Market,

mounds of freshly caught mackerel

thrash on a cement floor,

a desperate attempt to flee the morning

and its sharp edge of execution

for someone's culinary pleasure.

In the evening I turn

the tip of my last cigarette sunward

as the steel arch of the Brooklyn Bridge

burns way above Water Street,

marking the dream flesh of downtowners,

dreaming of fleeing nowhere.

Night of a New Yorker

At White Horse Tavern,

I face the refracted city light

through the amber of Guinness

with a well-toned crowd of young bodies,

way after Dylan Thomas

settled his score with the world.

His shade still hovers

over his portrait in the back room

as in the days of Mailer pounding

his manly convictions, or at night,

Delmore Schwartz reciting pages

from *Finnegan's Wake.*

As night deepens, four firemen saunter in

with boots caked in ash, helmets smoked.

A sudden fire of defiance rolls over sawdust.

Waitresses dance with firemen on tabletops,

strangers kiss and weep—

We are New Yorkers. We refuse to surrender.

The Way Things Ought to Be

When I walk past Wall Street,
the gaping holes don't bother me anymore.

Almost two years have passed.
I have learned to live with gaps and blank spaces,
as unclaimed scars of felt atrocities,
slowly the bent beams and charred sidings
are tucked away, letting a breathing spot
for dandelions rise like a rim of sun,
and men who built towers are planting
Dutch tulips with unshaken hands
and wind-dried eyes where children fly kites,
and a woman from Jersey raises money
for an orphan band, and the old rabbi
cracks jokes with his Black Muslim neighbor
about the permanence of stones,

and trains hustle, cracking dawn's shell.

Almost two years have gone by.

The gaps have started to seal,

and pomegranate seeds of congealed blood

are still strewn across the street as sad souvenirs.

Manhattan Mon Amour

The house near Gramercy Park

wrapped in Chinese silk of autumn dusk

cools and tucks inside.

While sipping baby-warm Darjeeling

and flipping through a Macy's catalog,

you talk about menarche, loneliness,

taxes, polygamy, de Kooning, and Castro.

I think about the times when the nearness

of you was a self-inflicted burn.

First you changed sides from the window to door,

then from East Side to West Side

and I followed.

You stopped loving parakeets and took to cats.

We grew older by days and somber by nights.

Now a square meter of perfumed space

separates our nights and the old man next door

always coughs at the ripe moment.

This is when you say, *In New York,*

each woman is a mirror

folding passion into fashion.

Art of Archery, Fear of Impregnation

Sometimes she likes to lead like fast-
moving water's pride
stinging cattle and singeing cornstalks.
On the barren field, desire stands stripped naked
like an orphan, helpless, teary-eyed.

Why can't I peel the skin and pierce the entrail
of New York? the boy asks with unforgiving eyes
as he sharpens the tip of an arrow on bare asphalt
hiding the shards of a fake romance.

At Central Park, titans wrestle, and their sweat
flows like a river of lazy illusion, painting
the sky in pink neon over empty armories,
wounded parakeets, and gaudy chandeliers.

All that he wants is Tribeca's angle,

Steppe of the Bronx, and the slopes of Queens,

like fragrant groves of mercy minus

the wealth embezzled in the secrets of slumming.

The girl paces in measured steps and

reaffirms her territory like a caged lioness

chooses not to choose water over her cave

and asks,

Do I still yearn for my virginity?

Non Finito

In paintings, I would like to see wind

blowing through oaks on the hill and

a woman at the creek gathering

ruins of her childhood, beauty-scented,

but I am neither a painter nor a curator

grappling with the tempting solidity of the unreal.

So, when I gazed, sitting behind the glass

of a café in Little Italy,

at the sight of a young girl,

speeding past on her roller skates,

I see the wind blowing.

Vinnie, the owner, smiled wisely—

you don't go to Rome to conquer;

you just treasure her splendor

and come back a little richer inside.

So much left undone by choice or chance—

a dinner missed in downtown,

a meeting in the Bronx, a hasty funeral

in Brooklyn, or a glimpse of past love

in a movie theater—never adding up to a whole.

Later at the Met, looking at rows of

paintings by old and modern masters

with scratched canvases, left-blank,

lazy strokes over green, under paint.

Dribbles of colors on lush bouquets

like trails of thoughts left visible.

O Non finito that

I long and seek after.

Looking for Mercy or November's Plight as It Unfolds

Beyond the ledge under a moon yet to rise, not too far

from sights and sounds of Brooklyn and the majestic

trouble just to get there in a streetcar named "Bridge Only",

sitting tight and alone like a pitchfork stuck in vine,

I watch the wide-eyed, close-lipped avenues down below.

Joneses have gone to Jones Beach and the Tylers

to their cute upstate bungalow before the winter's paws

prowl the land. My flanks are empty and quiet. My only light

shines at the Hudson as a lone Schopenhauer

looking at the timeless cat on his neighbor's back yard.

all wars are over, and stacks of silent guns deported elsewhere.

My wife of twenty-four years helps a Hippolyte rise

from a fall on the pavement of a distant town, always

Ms. Mercy bent over; face lit in a tender walk side by side

69

to a crowded bar, carrying the load of splintered years

and undoused, burning cinders, where she might encounter

another garrulous Gould cadging drinks—*I prefer gin but beer*

will do—then talking to seagulls; and I pass this eloquent silence

of a faceless evening lovesick and tired at the same time,

as a detangled tango dancer in the green room.

I hear the crowd gathering in ones and twos to rescue

a man high up, dressed for fall, now ready to jump

out of his world, the vaguely persuasive crowd passive

or passionate or just curious—hard to tell from my position.

Then the man falls and falls, gasping and unclasping O'Hara:

There is too much lime in the world and not enough gin.

Once Again

Looking for poetry in the city
can be pleasantly dangerous,
though not like looking for an antique bronze
in the Bronx in deep nights of the eighties.

But you can't simply stop looking—
as if ignoring water while swimming with sharks—
so, I found classrooms with walls painted pink,
empty halls of condemned buildings,
hastily built stages facing wooded avenues,
shaded balconies with carpentered stools,

until I stopped at the far end of East Fourth Street,
climbed a flight of stairs that ended in a darkened room
with bottles lined up against the wall
and memorabilia of the old communist regime—
a flag bearing hammer and sickle and a portrait of Lenin.

I was told I was in the KGB—

Kraine Gallery Bar.

Getting ready for a poetry reading:

a pleasant surprise or a

punitive soul searching?

No one was sure.

But there was

a heart-stopping silence—

Here (once again),

muses

leaving the gold.

Who's Afraid of Marianne Moore

For Dylan

Waiting in Shea Stadium,

for the game to begin,

the place to be in the mid-eighties.

Cold slap of the wind and embroidery

of a gauzy rain on the washed-out green

of autumn trees turning blue and orange

as evening seeps in.

With Gooden on the mound

and Strawberry screaming,

We own the town!

As streaming chariots in Olympia

in the service of Zeus,

naked athletes swerving in the air,

throbbing veins waiting to implode.

When bases are loaded

at the top of the inning,

an eloquent silence

runs in the veins.

Then cracking the ice of patience,

a swarm of wreathing wren

lifting with thunderous flaps

as faces in the gallery melt and

reconstitute as a crowd of clouds.

As the game ends, shouting feet

pass through dated turnstiles

into a night of fraternal forbearance.

Who's afraid of Marianne Moore?

Then they ride home and speak

to their children,

You will remember,

for we in our youth

did these things.

yes, many and beautiful things.

Barrow Street of the Mind

No books, no brow beating, no apocalyptic daybreak—

only the numbness of a run-over poplar in a snowstorm,

unfettered cobblestones of Water Street, where

a scream is reversed silence waiting for the ship

to arrive carrying the golden-haired lover from afar—

an Aztec, Norse, or Britton. Why does one care

at all when side rails are frozen over the Brooklyn

Bridge and an arctic despair diminish the sky

late under gaslight, as masked poets play and say

at every move, *Eliot is dead, long live Eliot?*

Dawn and Dusk at Seventy-First Street

As a child

pouring sand on sand

the huge piers of concrete below

try to screen the screaming day

from impossible nights.

Presidents, crooks, the toothless man

from an uptown shelter—

all visited the shrine and touched

the glare with bare hands.

But here the buck stops.

Underneath this catalpa's spread,

rock doves celebrate the Easter on the East Side,

and what is left becomes the fodder for the time machine.

Bystander's Query

New York is in its menopause now,

someone said in the N train to someone

while the girl sitting beside me like Buddha

plucked her eyebrows clean as a ballfield,

as I was getting ready to get out of the station.

I saw him the other day near

the Public Library,

where a little jazz, flavored with lamb soup,

wafted above the gardenia bush facing the lions

and a few pigeons, stubborn as mules,

peck at the letters on pages of *Post*

He always waits on the sidewalk,

here at the corner of Bleecker and Broadway,

keeps the paper on the wooden bench

as if for a friend, and smokes Maduro cigars

like a samurai in the royal garden.

I know exactly what he is going to do now.

He will look at his watch, fold the paper,

take out a tissue, blow his nose,

then amble to the door of Guys and Gals

and walk away with the same woman.

Miss Manhattan

How casually she lies on her bed in the park,

shaded by flowering lilacs, a few pigeons

nested in her folds, catnapping.

Her Grecian face half resting on nimble hands,

contained and content in reposed solitude.

For years, I have tried to turn

from her gaze,

yet she is all over—

atop monuments at the mouths of bridges,

guarding museums, flanking greeneries

of an obsolete past—

and the grandeur of her body softens

the sky almost to a whisper.

All I remember is her shedding clothes

and letting the butterfly out,

but no one has seen her shedding tears

afterward, or the sixty-five years of asylum-silence

that she rode on alone like a pure

drop of water borne to the sea on a lotus leaf—

only the gypsy fortuneteller

whispering in her younger ears a twisted future

and the hissing wind over Saint Lawrence River.

All she wanted, perhaps:

love's assurance, a few earthly comforts,

and the menacing voices of dark to disappear

in return for writing an ode to Beauty

with her body for a privileged city:

Among mortal women,

know this—

from every care, you could release me.

Adrift

Walking close, what you whispered
got scattered in the papery wind
hovering on wet spots on your tamarind
silk top like a thirsty bloodhound.

Here on McDougal Street, the meeting
of minds on women's rights
and socialist poetry hot off the press
under a sky loaded with flints.

Does it really matter what you ponder
and what you say or feel
when breast-stroking in the smoky air,
breathless to catch the spill
of buttered-cellophane wrapper's flutter
along your passionate ankles?

Maybe or maybe not.

Then you stride along summer's precipice

and gone as a wayward sun,

as I drift toward you like the proverbial

moth, and you spit fire to save me

from myself.

Morning Side Heights

Confounded, he puts his right foot first into the slush
of rapidly dissolving ice to latch onto the door handle
of his silver Chevy as he feels an opposing drag under
his left foot, that forces his upper torso to arch forward,
upsetting his balance: *I am going to fall flat on my face.*

Despite a quick jab of fright, he still sees the sky clearing
northwest of the tall sky hugger but somehow steadies
himself to a *thank God*, cursing hard instead at a
passing taxi spraying ice-cold, dirty water on the
beige tweed his ex-girlfriend gave him last Christmas.

Once inside the car, he feels stupid like his Moldovan friend
who thought Geena Davis had something to do with Gin
then he thinks it is about making
the right connections in whatever imagined ways,

to the wet earth and ask for her maternal support

and for some strange reason Andre Breton came to his mind:

Poetry is made in bed like love

On the Road to San Romano

Way back at the mouth of the river.

How lonesome one feels

walking along the edge of the river

on a threadbare road

wedged between the hangman's rock

and a desolate dock

with the descending sun and water still

as a body getting cold on a moonless night.

The city seems to be far away

with its faint sense of neon,

its distant murmur like a playground

getting filled with children,

and its humming bars on the West Side

with upright brigades of crafted bottles

and eyes wide shut.

As one walks and walks in passive steps,

windows blink like eyes at night.

Stars rest in peace under water.

Evening melts like butter in a pan.

Someone will remember us,

I say,

even in another time.

A Ferry Ride

On the shiny breast of undulating water,

a shadow, green and broken

the iconic Mother of Exiles.

The boat shifts in its passage.

we lean back on the seats in taut air

and clutch at the edge of our jackets.

There must be an Ellis Island in heaven,

you say *Yes,*

I nod, if there are

refugees of heart.

You smile, lavender scented.

In olive gardens beyond

the ultramarine shores

of Lesbos

immigrants become migrants,

and their despair runs the streets

as blood runs into sands.

How the words change their meaning

when you choose to be silent,

known becomes unknown.

Yet we know grief is not just a winch,

and a groggy, unkind night

may hurt less than a shrapnel day.

As the migrants wait near the gate,

their anger spreads in the chest

to guard against

a vainly barking tongue.

Now we have come full circle.

Stepping on the West Side Highway,

you say,

as you cut rosebushes harder,

they blossom more.

Grateful acknowledgement is made to the editors of the following publications where poems or versions of these poems first appeared. Sketches On Subway Steps: The Full Circle Journal (On Line) 2003, Sunset At Seaport Inn: Controlled Burn, Spring 2009, Black Out: Controlled Burn, Spring 2009, Night of A New Yorker: The Alembic, 2009, Bystander's Query: The Alembic, 2009, Side Street: Iodine Poetry Journal, Summer 2009, At The Tribeca Film Festival: Iodine Poetry Journal, Summer 2009, Pulse: Harpur Palate, Spring 2009 Unreal City: Common Ground Review 2016, Relief At Last: Common Ground Review 2016, A Sky NYPD Blue: Pennsylvania English 2016, The Way Things Are: The Round 2016, Who's Afraid Of Marianne Moore: Journal of NJ Poets 2017, A Ferry ride in the Circle Line: That September: Only here: East Jasmine review 2018.

My heartfelt and special acknowledgement to Ms. Ann Carson, whose illuminating translations of Fragments of Sappho has been inspirational in composing the following poems:

Only Here, The Cage, Reminder, Differing Accents, Hotel Chelsea of the Heart, Walking with Sappho in New York, Diagonal Descent, In a Gangster's den, Late spring, One Tattoo at a time,

Nonfinito, Once Again, Who's afraid of Marianne Moore Miss Manhattan, Way back at the mouth of the river, and Art of Archery, fear of Impregnation.

www.ingramcontent.com/pod-product-compliance
Lightning Source LLC
Chambersburg PA
CBHW030459130626
46549CB00007B/2781